AF584144

The First People lived together in groups. Aunties, uncles, and cousins all lived together.

Your aunty or uncle may look after you. Your mother and father were with you too!

Your mother would look after you. Your big mob of family would also look after you.

Your cousins and family would be friends too. They would live in the same group.

Your big family all know their culture. They live with the same beliefs.

Growing up meant getting ready to be men and women. You learned to hunt and gather food.

Learning how to make fire and spears was important. Children would play games throwing spears.

The stories of your culture were important. The stories were told to you by the older people.

Spear throwing was very important. You had to learn to hit the target.

To become a man you would be cut and marked. These cuts mean you are a man in the tribe. You are no longer a boy.

As a hunter you had to know how to track animals and spear them. Your job was important so everyone could survive.

Word bank

groups
aunties
uncles
cousins
mother
father
culture
beliefs
gathering
throwing
spears
stories
important
target
survive